All Worked Up

Ventings in Verse on
Corporate Life, Bosses,
Colleagues, and
Other Vexing Stuff

A. MARTIN BLOCK

DANIVIC PRESS

All Worked Up © copyright 2024 by A. Martin Block. All rights reserved. No part of this book may be reproduced in any form whatsoever, by photography or xerography or by any other means, by broadcast or transmission, by translation into any kind of language, nor by recording electronically or otherwise, without permission in writing from the author, except by a reviewer, who may quote brief passages in critical articles or reviews.

Danivic Press

Paperback ISBN: 979-8-9915543-1-2
Hardcover ISBN: 979-8-9915543-0-5

Cover illustration by Stuart McReath, Illozoo
Cover and book design by Jess LaGreca, Mayfly book design

Library of Congress Catalog Number: 2024919297
First Printing: 2024

For Paula, the source of everything great in my life

Disclaimer

I want to make one thing clear. These poems have **ABSOLUTELY NOTHING TO DO** with my current employer. They are about places I've worked and people I've known in **THE PAST**. The company I now work for is a beacon of efficiency, justice, compassion, and all that is right in corporate America. I have had no need, **NOR WILL I EVER NEED**, to write poems venting about my current employer or any of the fantastic people there.

Any perceived similarities between persons, operations, policies, and experiences about which I have written and those of my current employer are coincidental, unintended, wrong, and shameful misinterpretations that bring dishonor upon you and your entire family. Did I mention that these poems have **ABSOLUTELY NOTHING TO DO** with anyone or anything there?

To the board of directors and executive officers of my current company—non-retaliatory, exceptionally good-looking humanitarians that you are—kudos to you.

The people for whom, and with whom, I work day after day are **THE BEST**. I love my job and my utility providers would like me to keep it.

Introduction

In forty years as a lawyer with companies, law firms, and government, I, like you, have seen incompetence and myriad other aggravating behaviors honed to fine art. Early in my career, I identified four rational responses.

I could:

a. take them to heart, grow incensed and frustrated, and allow them to spike my blood pressure leading to premature death;

b. take them to heart, grow incensed and frustrated, and allow them to generate an ulcer requiring stomach surgery during which my blood pressure would spike leading to premature death;

c. take them to heart, grow incensed and frustrated, and allow them to cause a debilitating nervous disorder for which I would be prescribed powerful sedatives that, when combined with blood pressure medication, would lead to premature death; or

d. vent about them through mocking, amusing poetry.

I hope I made the right choice.

Contents

Disclaimer v
Introduction vii

Purpose

Purpose 3

My Kingdom for a Good Idea. Keep The Horse.
Perspectives and Practices of Organizational "Brain Trusts"

Relatively Speaking 7
Classified Ad for a Nepotism Hire 10
Shhh! 11
Substitution Theory 13
Woof! 14
You Can't Always Want What You Get 15

Risky Business 17
Disproportion 19
Whose Money is it Anyway? 20
"How Many Megaton, Sadie?" 23
Paper 24
Stop! Thief! 25
Making Lemonade 28
You Look Lovely This Evening 29
Listen, Grandchildren 32
Merger? 35

More People You Can't Choose

Bosses and Colleagues Who Make You Appreciate Family You Dislike

Bosses 39
Ode to a Born Leader 41
Sure, I'll Wait 43
This is Not Complicated 45
Religious Freedom 46
That Explains It 48
Colleagues 49
Status Quo, Holy Quo 53
Diagnosing Small Circle Syndrome 54
Numbers Don't Lie 57
A Tribute to Craig 59
My Turn 61
Haywired 63

Success in the Alternate Universe
Surmounting Aggravation More Often Than Never

Fill 'Er Up 67
Magic Time 68
Game Theory 69
Don't Ask Me. I Just Work Here 70
Let's Get Deep 72
Daylight 73
Perspective 75
Worth a Try 76
What Do You Mean I Can't Pay with This? 78
What Happened? 83
Money Matters 84
Yup, I Did That! 85
Yeah, Let's Go with That 89
One Approach 91

Office-Adjacent and Nonadjacent
Other Things That Need to be Said

A Good Day! 95
Battleground 96
Manifesto 98
Love Thyself 100
The Office Softball Dynasty 101
Metal Box 103
Let's Tie One On 104

The Motor Pool 109
Lunchroom 110
The Company Medical Office 113
Payback 116
Keep It to Yourself, Will Ya? 117
Who Cares? 119

You Want Jam on That?
You Want Jam on That? 123

Acknowledgments 125
About the Author 129

Purpose

Imagery is great and stringing words together fun,
but if you write a masterpiece, what, really, have you done?
Sure, you may have plumbed recesses of our shared condition,
compelled us into action through linguistic erudition,
sparked ideas, revealed love's worth, exalted nature's wonder,
by analogy and adverb driven apathy asunder.
I realize that's a point of art, a not-unworthy goal,
and I, as much as anyone, like grappling with my soul.
But even though enlightened, my existence has a quirk.
Although I'm on a higher plane, I have to go to work.
So I have deigned to remark on our all-too-common grind,
an exploration far more of the mindless than the mind.
Please read, recognize, and take heart, for in this book it's shown:
when you face stupid every day, you don't do it alone.

My Kingdom for a Good Idea. Keep the Horse.

Perspectives and Practices of Organizational "Brain Trusts"

Relatively Speaking

I joined a large financial firm
and within my first week,
the VP-Legal called and said,
"Alan, drop by. Let's speak
about a knotty lawsuit
with which we've just been served,
seeking six million dollars
that I'm sure are undeserved."

Handed the assignment,
I strategized and acted
to avert the liability
by which we'd be impacted.
And in only a few days,
by brilliant negotiation,
I attained stunning success
and personal elation.

I proudly told my boss
about the outcome I'd achieved.
I added that the C-suite
could feel thoroughly relieved
of all their genuine concern
about the risk extent,
as I had fought knowing the value
of each single cent.

I'd saved our company three mill,
half the sum demanded,
and with that the huge problem
soon could be fully remanded
to our lawsuit archive,
where it would rest in peace—
as soon as I got parties
to sign off on the Release.

He said, "Congratulations!
You had my confidence,
but three million bucks in this place
is of no consequence.
Three million dollars, to this firm,
is seen as constituting
a 'rounding error' at the most
and is not worth saluting."

I realized in those early days
my law school, though respected,
had taught something completely wrong,
leaving me misdirected.
My professor had told me
in my class on corporations,
the law sees them as "people"
as to rights and obligations.

But I recall my dad who worked
three jobs for eighty dollars,
never glimpsing the mindset
of those who wore white collars.

Companies can't be "people,"
whatever courts may say.
They're adversary species
sharing zero DNA.

Classified Ad for a Nepotism Hire

Loyalty not competence.
No need to question day one hence.
Regardless how inane or dense,
blind support must be immense.

Equivocation skills a must.
Positions should be firm as dust.
For baffling word salads may lust.
See clarity as act unjust.

Spelling skill need not be great.
Name one "alphabit" on your plate.
Name just one United State.
Have no desire to create.

Must be person void of shame.
Great pay, no work, should know whole name.
Should see advancement as a game
and ever seek others to blame.

Should abhor the phrase "to try."
Recognize the need to lie.
Must have morals we can buy.
Experienced? Need not apply!

Shhh!

There is a genius to the model of consulting firms
that for some tens of millions will, in no uncertain terms,
advise on how to optimize for growth and transformation,
to turn your stodgy enterprise into Wall Street's sensation.

Their genius isn't found in new ideas in which each traffics.
They sell recycled concepts merely juiced with modern graphics.
Their genius is identifying corporate boards' desires
to conceal their incompetence, and to that end, conspire.

When a company is mired or badly losing ground,
its board needs to show shareholders it has plans bold and sound
to energize the company and quell disgruntled factions.
So it retains consultants as a pretense to real action.

And the consultants hired examine old incarnations
of even older sales pitches and brand them "innovations,"
sell them to conspirators at vast, outrageous cost,
plus even more to implement—no profit margin lost.

Five years ago consultants sold a surefire advancement:
cubes instead of offices for guaranteed enhancement
of work collaboration, efficiency, engagement.
Destroy all the workplace walls, a brilliant new arrangement.

But that's already failing and we're hearing their "new" notions,
like private meetings in buildings to stoke business promotion.
They're calling for enclosed spaces where in-depth thought can flower.
Perhaps we'll call them "offices"—now that's sure to empower.

All parties know the plans won't work and cannot drive results.
They've failed before, or mattered not, nothing here to exult.
It simply is repackaging of what has come before,
a fact every conspirator finds useful to ignore.

So when you see this farce play out at work or in the news,
watch for, among the telltale signs, the most telling of clues:
the emptier the verbiage by which plans are conveyed,
the greater the sum being trashed, the more that board's afraid.

Substitution Theory

I can't eat office furnishings. Chairs are hard to chew,
and laptops are a bit too tough to get my teeth into.
I can't deposit carpeting in my checking account,
and a big desk or bookcase won't enhance my cash amount.
A paint job in my office may be pleasing to the eye,
but it won't help me at the store with what I want to buy.

The boss says smart surroundings are in lieu of greater pay,
that with a nice environment for less cash we should stay.
A miniature paycheck should bring glee to us we're told,
because of office décor we are *privileged* to behold.

If this guy truly believes his substitution theory,
let him practice all the talk of which I've grown so weary.
His own office accoutrements are comfort to excess.
He'd better cut his own pay or hypocrisy confess.

Somehow I feel his theory would lose all of its appeal
if he who preached it had to down a desk lamp for a meal.

Woof!

I have it on good authority that a few years ago
our firm made it priority to restrict people flow
and ensure the unauthorized could not get to our floors,
guaranteeing they're turned back right at our building doors.

They spared no expense to shield people and information,
installing a foolproof defense to safeguard each workstation.
No longer would those ne'er-do-wells so easily gain entry.
For now we had an eagle-eyed, unhoodwinkable sentry.

Defenders guard our complex, let no outsiders pass.
They act with lightning reflex, just steps from our front glass.
People seeking access now show photo IDs,
and turnstiles are unlocked only for staff and invitees.

But recently I have learned the system's not so tight.
It is a source of real concern of which I'll not make light.
It seems that for more than a month a colleague, name of Daniel,
had used an ID, for a laugh, that showed his cocker spaniel.

And no one ever questioned Dan as each day without fail,
he moved about most easily, despite no wagging tail.
He revealed our security has some substantial flaws,
since no one ever noticed he was lacking all four paws.

So if you intend trouble at our home office compound,
there's no need to be subtle when you choose to come around.
Rest assured our security scarcely will take note
and only tell police that the perp had a glossy coat.

You Can't Always Want What You Get

Our cubicles all are arrayed in neat parallel lines,
and every five and one-half feet our names appear on signs.
At 8 a.m. we walk among space modular and blank
and sit before computer screens with others of our rank.

Is this how I'm to live my days, in this small universe
that is a clone of untold more? The Big Bang in reverse?
Has there been a divine decree of which I've not been told,
directing I remain walled in until I'm dead or old?

I do admit a comfort in my coffin-like surround,
with colors that are neutral and fabrics that absorb sound,
I must concede a peace of mind knowing Cube Thirty-three,
at least until I'm fired, will, kind of, belong to me.

It may be tiny, windowless. It may be spartan bare.
It may be utilitarian, but it's mine when I'm there.

And then I glimpse the other world for winners of the race.
Where offices and dining rooms occupy special space.
Where higher-ups prop high their feet and shut their doors to nap.
The realm for keepers of the cubes, designers of the map.

But I'm not jealous. I'm not mad. For in my heart I know,
in the next corporate merger they will be the first to go.
Their salaries are burdensome, their pensions even more.
Surely a new management will show their rears the door.

And maybe then, when that day comes, I'll finally get my due.
I'll snare a big promotion and vast riches will ensue.
I'll move myself way down the hall into a lofty perch,
trading my fake Formica for a desk of seasoned birch.

Ah! Then I will enjoy my life, and have the things I want:
respect and cars and bank accounts and lessers I can taunt.
I'll buy a house so grand and tall, by great chandeliers lit,
with rooms so vast that in them these damned cubicles would fit.

I'll have arrived and, at long last, have left this life behind.
Then I'll get canned and lose it all. I forgot. Never mind.

Risky Business

Business decisions carry risk. It really doesn't matter
whether you're sitting atop, or down, the corporate ladder.
Each step and direction may result in loss or gain.
Each action and reaction could bring profit or cause pain.

For every single enterprise, risk is a basic fact.
And that is why each day, each person considers the impact
on the financial bottom line of everything they do,
all results, long-term or short, that one day may ensue.

Academic disciplines breed company success—
business, law, accounting, more, are drivers of progress.
Education, expertise are valued in those spheres
and are common determinants of successful careers.

But there's one so-called discipline that simply is not real.
It is a made-up, phony field designed just to conceal
that it is void of substance. There's no science, no art,
an alleged branch of learning with no value to impart.

"Risk Management" it calls itself, becoming all the rage.
Boards cynically appease Wall Street, bringing it center stage.
Regulators think it shields against unwise decisions,
and business schools provide degrees simply to boost tuition.

The risk management complex, though, while useless, is quite clever.
It makes itself seem critical to the business endeavor.
It creates charts, analyses, graphs, "profiles" galore.
It even, laughingly, tags risks from level 1 to 4.

Practitioners in this "field" are paid sizeable sums,
to act as if they "quantify" all possible outcomes.
They report meaningless "measures" to boards and senior folk,
while serving no real function. They're all in on the joke.

So if you're struggling as you choose a path for your career,
whether just out of college or exploring new frontiers,
and seek merely to repeat things that others have foreseen,
make up empty numbers and pretend to insights glean,

I recommend risk management. It is the perfect path:
numerical analysis with no basis in math.
Each day you will be praised as you recite obvious threats.
It won't be satisfying, but it will help pay your debts.

Now to ensure advancement, let me be your guide.
There is but one essential rule by which you must abide.
Despite compelling evidence, never make the concession
that your chosen career is not an actual profession.

Disproportion

I find it most ironic
that companies iconic
would pay their CEOs such absurd, outrageous sums,

as if they're football players
or boxing champion slayers,
while their primary skill is endless flapping of their gums.

When most of their decisions
are mere fodder for derision
by their customers, shareholders, and employees alike,

as from a corner palace,
they feign concern while acting callous,
dreading the day the board and Wall Street types say "Take a hike!"

Imagine distribution
of that income. Retribution!
Real cash going to all the folks who actually do work.

Base company advancement
on contributor enhancement
and stop rewarding many who are well-connected jerks.

Whose Money is it Anyway?

There is one thing most crucial,
one essential task,
to be performed with skill and speed.
Need you even ask
what the vital act may be,
so high above them all?
It is the act of being paid,
in dollars large or small.

So why is this critical job
so often screwed up so?
As if through heads at payroll
ancient mighty rivers flow,
through caverns hollowed by the force
of years of nature's rage,
that with each calculation
reduce concern for your wage.

We speak here not of politics or pride
or of promotion.
We speak here of survival—
that's why the big commotion.
Whose money is it anyway
that, despite the amount,
they act as if it's coming
from their personal account?

Payroll dodders at their desks.
They just don't seem to care
if you go weeks without your pay
and pull out all your hair.

It is a form of cruelty,
surely against the law.
An uncaring futility
leaving nerves frayed and raw.

Somehow I bet payroll folks
get their checks right on time,
as if an hour's odd delay
would be federal crime.

There is but one solution
to problems of being paid,
to inhuman recurrence
of survival's means delayed.

Rotate jobs within this place.
Let each one have their turn
to be in charge of check output
and move quick as a fern.

Then every payroll staffer
would liven up their pace,
as fear would vitalize their numbing
number-laden space.

Introduction to "How Many Megaton, Sadie?"

In 1980, during my first week with the legal department of the New York City Board of Education at its Brooklyn headquarters, while at my assigned spot in a hallway next to the men's room, I was poking around in my antiquated desk. There I found something remarkable: a 1955 New York City Board of Education Civil Defense Manual.

The pamphlet's most enlightening pages gave instructions for employees to follow in the event of nuclear attack on Brooklyn. It directed employees, immediately after a bombing, to, among other things, estimate the size of the bomb, identify the precise location where the bomb fell, and then phone, that's right, *phone* the information into Board of Education headquarters. All I can say is thank goodness New York City had installed nuclear concussion-proof telephone poles, radiation-resistant rotary dials, and, most importantly, non-melting operators.

Another section of the handbook detailed a chain of command of Board of Education personnel. It told employees whom to call with bomb information in the event senior commanders, who moments ago had been superintendents and principals, were killed. Only with recent revelations that the Russians were developing pomposity-seeking bombs can we fully appreciate the danger senior Board of Education officials were facing.

It may not be coincidence that in 1955 Albert Einstein died and I was born, resulting in a breathtaking net loss of intelligence within the human population. The Board of Education's Civil Defense Manual is Exhibit A.

Here is a conversation apparently anticipated by the prescient planners who authored the manual.

"How Many Megaton, Sadie?"

"How many megaton, Sadie?"
"Maybe about forty," said Rose.
"It was clearly a big one," said Sadie,
"but just how big it was—who knows?"
"What did it land on?" Rose asked.
Sadie said, "That's hard to fix."
Rose pressed, "I need know exactly."
Sadie said, "Room 206."
"But what building was it?" asked Sadie.
Rose countered with "Let's just say,
a walk-up somewhere in Queens Village,
that has seen a much better day."
Then Rose looked up the next directive
in her Civil Defense Handbook.
It said she should call the field general,
promoted from a lunchroom cook.
So Sadie called up her commander,
to tell her the megaton peak,
while Rose made a hairdresser appointment
for her nephew's bar mitzvah next week.

Paper

I can't produce more paper.
The copy machine just broke.
I tried to produce more paper,
but the damn thing started to smoke.
I know I need more paper.
Forty copies won't suffice,
all destined for the trash heap
at environmental price.
If you submit mounds of paper,
our board will value concede,
for volume is persuasive
to folks too lazy to read.

Stop! Thief!

We are told employee theft will leave corporate profits bereft,
a major threat about which we are warned.
They say it's just a few bad types conducting frequent brazen swipes.
Those colleagues must be hunted, shunned, and scorned.

They tell us our office supplies, and this does come as a surprise,
on the black market fetch a handsome sum.
Apparently, our legal pads are fenced criminally by the scads,
while the good folks around us remain mum.

Our pens and our tan folders, our plastic report holders,
are disappearing every day with ease.
Our Post-its and our markers. Damn you, you Ma Barkers,
with your cunning and your heisting as you please!

They say this epidemic has made our enterprise sick,
and steadily company health declines.
With so much being purloined, we're aggressively enjoined
to be alert to all possible signs.

I clearly get the import and see that I must report.
It means business survival, I agree.
Let's end the days of plunder and throw the thieves asunder
and make it crystal clear our stuff's not free.

But I should not be aghast as I recall my own past.
I must look both behind and up ahead.
I cannot sit idly by, cognizant that I lie
about the all too evil life *I've* led.

I finally admit it. Until now I have hid it.
I'll not abide this guilt another day.
I feel disgraced and ashamed, deserving to be defamed.
I will resign and so your fears allay.

It was I, I confess. I'm why we're in this whole mess.
I'm why the company will go bankrupt.
I'd no idea, I swear it, but I'll no longer bear it.
How could I be so hopelessly corrupt?

My technique I perfected, so you never suspected.
I am the reason for our sinking ship.
You placed all your trust in me, but in 1983,
I took home a middle-sized paper clip.

I'll face incarceration and rehabilitation.
I'll pray that you forgive me for my sin.
Don't stigmatize my children. I'm not a man among men.
I'm why we're in the crisis that we're in.

And to executive staff, I'm sure you'll have a good laugh
picturing me in my prison vault.
I'm why you are insolvent, and so badly overspent.
There's just no way this collapse was *your* fault.

So you'll not wait a moment to fire up some foment,
distracting from the truth to guard your fate.
Your corporate P.R. expert, doubtless, will rush to assert
the cause of your demise: Paper Clip–Gate!

But I'll have satisfaction and get the last reaction,
in prison write my memoir as I rot,
and submit for publication, ultimate retaliation,
with pages bound together by—guess what?

Making Lemonade

Take Your Daughter to Work Day,
a great innovation for girls planning their careers.

And it worked in its own way
to propel imagination, showcase once-foreclosed frontiers.

The day could be exciting,
impressing with your slot amid the hectic office din.

The chance was so inviting,
if you were an astronaut, or something else akin.

But a job ordinary,
soon will render progeny feeling bored and aggrieved.

Reactions will not vary,
as their eyes mirror sadness for so much you've not achieved.

But though they seemed deflated,
daughters were inspired to go kick in all the doors.

They emerged dedicated
to never be so mired, and desperate to pursue *every* career other than yours.

You Look Lovely This Evening

If you're a corporate manager, make sure you know the lingo.
Use it at every meeting until attendees think, "Bingo,
our card of corporate speak is full, proving we're productive.
Knowing this new language is exciting and seductive."

To give but one example, before I would proceed,
some time ago I might have said, "Let's all get up to speed"
or maybe take a moment to get folks "on the same page."
But every meeting now starts with a phrase that's all the rage.

The opening required at the outset of all sessions,
to ensure peak efficiency, avert needless regressions,
is "Okay, everybody, it's time to *level set*."
Though that sounds idiotic, there's one stupider yet.

If someone has an idea, concept, or innovation,
a notion that, if acted on, could be a great sensation—
but also, just as easily, bring reproachment and dread—
there is a precondition 'fore the notion moves ahead.

You're told to "socialize it," that's the term of art you hear.
It is an odd way to assess your confidence or fear.
For if you "socialize it," it may be loved or hated,
and, crucially, those not objecting will be implicated.

They tell me it's mandated to gauge my idea's potential,
assuring me I will become respected, influential.
Now being the literal sort, I need no further clue.
If you are told to "socialize it," here's what you must do.

Get to know your idea in a real and profound way.
Find out its favorite color. See what it has to say.
Meet it for cappuccino, perhaps take in a show.
Discern its likes and dislikes, for only then you'll know.

Learn each other's views on life. Discover your shared passions.
Seek out its sense of humor and observe its chosen fashions.
Impress it with your intellect. Always converse politely.
Show your idea a good time. Make sure you're not unsightly.

Ask it what its sign is. Talk politics, religion.
Get its sense of the day's news, the future it envisions.
Instigate some banter. See how quick its mind.
Explore both history and art. Who knows what you will find?

A movie's a nice outing and might stir conversation
to check if you're compatible or destined for abrasion.
Perhaps you'll hold your idea's hand—that's always a nice touch.
And buy a popcorn, large or small. Your idea won't eat much.

Take in a ballgame or go dancing. Either one is fun.
Perhaps a walk along the beach when a long day is done.
And if you sense connection, ask the idea to dine.
Share a candlelit dinner featuring aged steak and wine.

But one quick note of caution as you share that fancy food—
don't be derailed by others in the restaurant staring, rude.
For though they'll think you're toasting, laughing with an empty chair,
you and you alone will know your idea sits right there.

And if you both determine neither wants to be alone,
meet the idea's family, and have it meet your own.
Perhaps there'll be a wedding yielding untold happy days,
and maybe cute little ideas will come along to raise.

I'm sure that's what "socialize" means, the obvious intention
of the command that follows every new idea that's mentioned.
I might be wrong, but if I am, with my interpretation,
at least you'll have companionship midst your humiliation.

Listen, Grandchildren

There once were things called "offices"
into which masses streamed,
dragging themselves from houses,
on scarce rest and troubled dreams.

Clustered in edifices,
piled high floor over floor—
some were half-open boxes,
some even had a door.

And, oh, the daily frenzy
was a great sight to behold.
Furnace of economics
where people, routine, grew old.

Filing and calculating,
writing memos and such.
Feverish activity
that did not amount to much.

Civilly pretending,
deferring based on rank,
to see alternate Thursdays
a deposit to your bank.

I kid you not, grandchildren,
work and home were apart:
one for tasks you just abide,
one for tasks of the heart.

Then came the new computing,
devices in your hand.
An "interconnectivity"
so many thought so grand.

And you could work from anywhere.
In fact, not could, but must.
Relentless reachability,
the new yardstick of trust.

Chasm obliterated.
Work can't wait. Be "on tap."
For wheresoever you may be,
there's high-res in your lap.

Companies soon realized
footprints could be downsized.
Why pay for *any* workspace
if home-work is maximized?

They created a new concept,
dubbed it "work mobility."
But pajamas were no antidote
for stress, futility.

Remember consequences.
Most things come at steep cost.
Offices may be extinct,
but more than they were lost.

When online in wee hours,
and for lost sleep you grieve,
know the bargain ceded
the one goal it could achieve.

While there is real advantage
foregoing commuter dash,
recall the driving factor here:
employers' drive for cash.

For while they make more money,
you work longer for yours.
Work did not give way for life.
Life yielded to work chores.

It must seem so ironic
to the naively inclined.
A scheme promoting balance
has that balance undermined.

For though they shed your office,
your working space increased.
Your office became the planet,
and *you're* paying for the lease.

Merger?

They said it was a merger.
They said it would be great.
They said careers would blossom,
and good things we'd await.

"Opportunity" the watchword.
A new global playground.
A stage as large as Earth itself,
yes, potential unbound.

We've become a big player,
worldwide fourth in size.
How much our incomes would balloon
we scarcely could surmise.

All our daily efforts
would now multiply the yield.
We'd finally made the major leagues.
Our bright futures were sealed.

Next day they cut our benefits,
axed everyone we knew,
and made us feel as if we were
stuff stuck beneath their shoe.

They transferred us around the town,
pushed us here and there,
until it fully dawned on us,
they wanted us nowhere.

They dubbed it "fiscal soundness."
People must be released.
While all the while they made quite sure
their friends' prospects increased.

Units were "independent,"
but in the settling dust,
it soon became quite clear
they meant independent of us.

They said they knew the best approach,
called our ways "second rate."
An unrelenting arrogance
that ever sealed our fate.

They said it was a merger.
That cannot be denied.
They said we'd all be better off.
They said a lot. They lied!

More People You Can't Choose

Bosses and Colleagues Who Make You Appreciate Family You Dislike

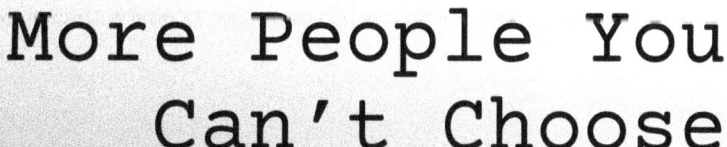

Bosses

Every few years, people between ages ten and twenty-five coin a word or phrase to denote something admirable. Over the last seventy years alone, we've seen, in no particular order, "rad," "phat," "awesome," "neat," "cool" (sometimes followed by "daddio"), "dope," "sick," "far out," "righteous," "hip," "groovy," "fly," "gnarly," "wicked," "sweet," "fire" and a whole lot more I was never "hep" enough to understand. In the early twentieth century, people often voiced favorable sentiment by referencing cats wearing pajamas and bees having knees. (It probably is no coincidence those phrases disappeared from the lexicon immediately after Coca-Cola removed cocaine from its formula.)

For me, growing up in Queens in the mid-1960s, the word was "boss." I have no idea where it came from or how widely it was used. At times I've thought the word may have spread only to the end of my street. People my age seem to have no recollection of it and think I'm weird for asking if they do.

Everything exceptional was "boss." That ballgame was boss. That rock band was boss. That doughnut was boss. That new shirt was boss. Often, we tacked on "man," as in "That is so boss, man." Calling something "boss" was to provide our ultimate seal of approval.

Only when I entered the workforce did I realize how misguided our use of the term had been. "Boss" does not mean something great. In the real world, it denotes something bad (used here to mean "bad" and not to mean "good" in the way people in the mid-'80s tried to get us to understand the meaning of "bad" during the only Opposite Day in history that lasted five years). There is a reason the dictionary defines "boss" as "one who most likely is incompetent, self-centered, lazy, irrational and/or unintelligent, but who, nonetheless, has been granted absolute authority over other human beings."

If I could go back, I'd tell my ten-year-old self to stop calling so many things "boss" and come up with another word. Perhaps we should have said things were "laudable," as in "That car is so laudable, man" and reserved "boss" for what it is: a person who, although inferior to you in every important way, still gets to tell *you* what to do and judge *your* worth.

That is just so not laudable, man.

Ode to a Born Leader

Late in the evenings and into the morns,
thoughts of the day ahead prod me like thorns.
Needling anxiety in my heart and mind,
as my boss on his shoulders transports his behind.

I must not dwell on the office tonight.
The darkness is sacred. There's time in the light
to ponder and fathom with wonder profound
how this place could be managed by this lifeless mound.

Perhaps he is not marked by ineptitude.
Perhaps he's brilliant but always misconstrued.
Perhaps he'll reveal his worth any day soon.
Perhaps I am really the Man in the Moon.

No, I'm not mistaken. It's writ on his face.
His depositing paychecks? Unholy disgrace.
He hides at his desk like a child in mom's skirt,
praying the day's events leave him unhurt.

But how can we end this long reign of malaise
that radiates down from that man in a daze?
All we can do is keep doing our best
and hope, at some point, there's an ultimate test.

A test that will prove to the world what we know,
that each thought impulse is painstakingly slow.
That shows there is nothing he cares much about,
a test that undoubtedly vanquishes doubt.

A challenge on which he'll dramatically fail,
compelling his own boss to finally bail
and hire a person possessed of some vision.
A person willing to make one damned decision!

Sure, I'll Wait

I hate it when my phone rings and promptly I am told
some exec is calling and that I should please hold,
followed by wasted minutes sitting silent, idly by,
awaiting worthless words from some self-adulating guy.

Who the hell does he think he is, directing me to wait?
A span designed solely to say "You're worthless, but I'm great."
Having me suspend in space upon that message terse,
pausing all thought and action until he deigns to converse.

Who is he to think his time more valued than my own?
Manipulating me to wait for his anointed tone
and using his assistant to advance his venal game,
as if invoking fear by the mere mention of his name.

What would be the best response to his insulting tack?
To just hang up and hit voicemail at every rude callback?
Or should I just do nothing, endure the intended slight,
fated to stew about it through another sleepless night?

Or when his eminence comes on, should I be more base
and say how dearly I would like to rearrange his face?
Or maybe I should tell him his pathetic sport is blown,
suggest his fingers leave his nose and learn to use a phone.

No, I think none of those the most appropriate reply,
as pity more than anger is what I feel for this guy.
Imagine someone so unsure about his place on earth,
he's driven to such inane stunts in search of some self-worth.

No, I will not be nasty. His game already failed.
His ego is not serviced, his bolstering derailed.
For while we two don't think alike, there's one thing we both see:
for all his self-delusion, he had to talk to me.

This is Not Complicated

Subject matter expertise is not qualification
for movement into management and corporate elevation.
Likewise, more seniority is not a real credential
when looking for a leader who's effective, consequential.
Having friends or relatives ensconced in the C-suite
will not ensure discernment that's good for the balance sheet.
And choosing someone who's willing to work at reduced rate
will not promote a corporate culture to which folks relate.
To keep your top contributors from turning tail and fleeing,
just make sure each manager is a decent human being.

Religious Freedom

All people worship differently toward images diverse.
Most prefer an entity with which they can converse.
Many, as in ancient day, found sculpted sandstone holy.
Others look within themselves for consolation solely.

But I work for a man who worships unlike all the rest.
He finds devout communion and while others sneer and jest,
this man will plummet to a knee and, overcome with awe,
adore his sovereign with a zeal I've never seen before.

He does not worship icons of divinity removed.
He does not pray to monarchs or to forest life behooved.
He finds ecclesiastical not what is seen, but heard.
He revels in the sound of *the vocabulary word*.

But not all Webster's entries can evoke the sacred feel.
Most are to him but empty, shallow, meaningless, unreal.
Only nouns, not verbs or else, can so arouse his soul.
And not all nouns are suited for his sacramental role.

He finds "cannoli" holy and is wrought by "ham on rye."
While some worship a shepherd, this guy worships "shepherd's pie."
Even the word "pudding" never fails to make him quake.
He thinks the gospel spreading when he hears of "angel cake."

But as in most religion, one true light commands his will,
and in his unique dogma there's "a city on a hill."
Yet I simply could not fathom the word he most revered,
the word whose sound is that toward which his saintly life is steered.

And then, by chance, it happened. I learned his shining light.
Suddenly he shook and cried, awash in joy and fright.
It was in an elevator, people were chatting free,
when all at once, without warning, he crumpled to a knee.

He quivered there, staring aground, afraid to lift his head.
And then a calm subdued his angst. *But what had someone said?*

I replayed those crucial moments in my mind as if on tape,
searching for the word that left his mouth and soul agape.
And then I caught it, clear as glass, the truly sacred sound,
so mighty that where'er he is wild fervor is unbound.

A woman told another how she'd spent the afternoon.
She spoke about the office pace and the stock market boon.
And as she spoke about a meal she'd had that very day,
the zealot fell enraptured when he heard the word "buffet."

So then I knew the holy sound, the force from which he sips.
The utterance he endless prays will grace his dying lips.
Now, when he starts to denigrate my value in the least,
I mention lunch, and speak "the word," and he thinks I'm his priest.

That Explains It

Elemental, disconnectal, psychotime condition,
is what our manager displays with the further addition
of assontonic, jerkatoidal, manipuloid layover.
Management by weirdity, a world you must discover.

Tirades are wholly unprovoked, but make sense in his mind.
You grow angry and sullen as day to day you find
you hate yourself for staying, for yielding to abuse.
You rage against insanity, but find you can't cut loose.

The unforeseen is commonplace, all colors are reversed.
The wrong is true, the right is left, bizarreness unrehearsed.
Each task you do is short of mark, decisions ruled inept
by he for whom you toil each day, he of sense bereft.

And you, you fear, will fade in time, your sanity erased.
You'll start to lose all sense of self, or fix on time and space.
But then a small voice near your ear halts your fated flight.
Rod Serling tells you where you are and everything's alright.

Colleagues

Great colleagues are interesting, funny, thoughtful, conversational, supportive, and friendly. They help us cope with problematic bosses. They're the people we genuinely miss after they've been fired for embezzlement. Unfortunately, other colleagues enhance our stress, just by being themselves.

Etymology of the word "colleague" gives us insight into these complex working-world relationships. Etymology, of course, is the study of word origins. This is not to be confused with entomology, the study of things gross and terrifying. As I began writing this section, I had no intention of discussing insects. They have no relevance to colleagues. Yet here we are.

I appreciate the value of some insects. I acknowledge the critical contributions honeybees make to our ecosystem, the consistency of sticky buns, and the population's soaring A1C levels. I also am okay with honeybees because, typically, they mind their own business. The same cannot be said of others in the insect category I call "expectedly airborne." Take wasps and hornets, of the murdering variety or not: creatures plainly uninterested in peaceful coexistence. They enter your home uninvited, plunge at you as if *you* were the trespasser, and then lack the courtesy to leave, irrespective of how many doors and windows you open.

In all insect categories, the larger the creature, the more terrifying it is. There is one notable exception to this rule of scale: Mothra. Mothra may topple skyscrapers with a flap of its wings, but it at least has the decency to never sneak into your living room.

The second insect category is the "expectedly groundborne." Having grown up in New York City, I am very familiar with these crawling, multi-legged, tentacled monsters—the ones that could strut around Jurassic Park without attracting a second glance from other prehistorics.

The third category is the "unexpectedly airborne." They are most horrifying of all. Exemplar of this ghastly set is the cicada. Though as large as canoes, and as aerodynamic as sofabeds, they, nonetheless, have flight capability.

Cicadas have cornered the market on hellish. Not only do they emerge from the bowels of the earth, they do so in swarms, creating the disturbing impression that structures you know to be fixed are moving. Throughout their thankfully short lives, they hover menacingly above our heads mocking us with clicks, buzzes and whooshes. Even in the throes of death, after dropping from trees onto sidewalks and fields, they have a final act of treachery in store. Without warning, they leap onto innocent passersby to ensure their time amongst us is remembered because, apparently for them, a billion offspring is not sufficient legacy.

But I digress.

The word "colleague" derives from "coll," meaning grouping. The stem portion, "league," also is the stem of "beleaguered." So, according to etymologists, "colleagues" are groups of people by whom one feels beleaguered. That sounds right.

Do you remember taking essay exams? (I bet those little blue booklets still haunt your nightmares.) Do you remember writing your opening paragraph setting out your position, and then supporting and summarizing that position? Do you remember, on occasion, as you got deeper into the writing, you realized the points you were making argued more effectively for the position opposite the one you had asserted so resolutely at the outset?

Well, I've done it again. I may have been hasty in asserting entomology has no relevance to colleagues. After all, many of them really bug me.

This page is intentionally left blank.[*]

[*]The International Code of Corporate Conduct requires this appear at least once.

Introduction to "Status Quo, Holy Quo"

You know how, at the end of those day-long company conferences, you often receive a lovely parting gift? I've received books about success, business, success in business, and the business of success, as well as lapel pins, mugs, and pens. One time each attendee received an oversized company stock certificate made entirely of low-quality chocolate. (Sadly, its value exceeded that of the company's actual stock.)

My favorite "thanks for being here" gift was a paperweight heavy enough to withstand hurricane-force winds—because, apparently, in a hurricane, your primary concern should be keeping pages of your memos orderly. It was metal and looked like a giant coin about five inches in diameter. Across the paperweight was emblazoned the inspirational message "CHANGE IS GOOD!" From every presentation to which we'd been subjected that day, you might have thought inclusion of the second "O" in "GOOD" was a typo.

"CHANGE IS GOOD!" My colleagues and I assumed the message referred to opportunities for career enhancement sure to come our way following the next corporate reorg. The following March we realized it actually was preparation for the size of our annual bonus.

Status Quo, Holy Quo

Status quo, holy quo,
why is it they love you so?
Why do thoughts of some progress
put them under such duress?
Why is it reform they fight?
Why is movement never right?
Why does action firm or sure
seem to them an act impure?
Why do they so fear to grow?
Why is everyone so slow?
Why is it each night they pray
to live again their yesterday?
Why is sameness so revered
that toward its mark their lives are steered?
Why do they resist the new
as if plotted by a maddened few?

Status quo, holy quo,
why is it they love you so?
Could it be that change, they know,
would soon reveal they had to go?

Diagnosing Small Circle Syndrome

A subset of populations, often those of wealthy stations,
have a medical condition unlike all other disease.

The differentiating factor, the litmus-like reactor,
is that those around them suffer while *they* bear it with great ease.

Even more mysterious is that they are oblivious
to even being ill, as they amble through their days.

And yet it is a fact that those with whom they interact
are victimized by the sickness in countless, profound ways.

It's called Small Circle Syndrome. It comes from their childhood home.
It causes them to see the universe smaller than most.

For them, it's a tiny realm in which they command the helm,
a game show they let others play, but never let them host.

Victims all are fated to see only those related
by blood to them as sentient and, therefore, worth a damn.

You don't share their DNA? You are worthless. Go away!
While their exploits are riveting, your presence is a sham.

Luckily, however, the main symptom, the bellwether,
can readily be diagnosed by any non-physician.

And when the telltale's spotted, you can, by time allotted,
reduce your own exposure to the dangerous condition.

Engage in any brief chat, and if you soon realize that
whatever subject you advance, despite seeming convivial,

they pivot the discussion and, with relentless percussion,
regale you with personal news, however wildly trivial.

If you find yourself relating how horrid and devastating
you find a loss of life or peril people must endure,

you're met with consternation, and their own tragic frustration,
over next week's concert tickets they're unable to secure.

If you raise a work topic, their focus is myopic.
You'll learn of some extravagant, but pointless, acquisitions.

If you mention it's raining, you'll be met with complaining
that planning glam vacations demands exhausting decisions.

If they ask after your child, please, please do not be beguiled.
Anything you proffer they most promptly will ignore.

They only feign attention so they're then prompted to mention
what their own kids are up to, for there's no way *that* could bore.

If you see this worrying sign, step back and, yes, you'll be fine.
You'll know how to be safe in any future face-to-face.

Just realize from the outset that you're only just an outlet
for news on those who, unlike you, exist in time and space.

Introduction to "Numbers Don't Lie"

People who not only think appearance correlates to value, but also believe they have a right to rate another's appearance, are among the lowest of the low. To the extent beauty even is a thing, everyone has it, and everyone should see it in everyone else.

But human nature dictates that each of us assess our appearance in the hope others will find us physically attractive. That is why the mirror and puddle were invented. Most of us look at our reflected image and realistically assess our attractiveness. Some greatly underestimate it. And then there are those who wildly overestimate it. You know them. You've worked with them. You've secretly laughed at them. And you are right to do so.

Numbers Don't Lie

Corporate life is replete with figures, graphs formulaic,
streaming analytics, computations archaic,
EPS and ROEs and P/E ratios,
market caps, yields, dividends, targets for CEOs.
But there's another datum that's not typically reported:
degrees to which the self-image of colleagues is distorted.

It's called Appearance Number, and it isn't really new.
It calculates deltas between divergent points of view.
It quantifies the gap between what you and others see
when you see your reflection and they encounter thee.
You need not have an A in trig or advanced numbers theory.
All you need is eighth-grade math, simple algebra really.

So with an X, a Y, and Z comes the basic equation,
$X - Y = Z$. Here's a demonstration.
If X stands for the value you yourself give your appearance,
near zero if just "okay." Ten, magnetic adherence.
And Y tells us how others rate the way they think you look—
zero if you disgust them and ten if their breath you took.
Just plug into the formula, solve for Z and find
your image/real world calculus, the truth of your own mind.

If Z's a number close to ten, your status is "No Peer."
It means that on Earth you alone think heaven sent you here.
If it comes out negative ten, you have the "Get a Grip."
It means people think you're just fine, but you think you're a drip.
If Z's a number in between, it means you sense correctly.
You see yourself as others do. You are healthy, abjectly.

We work with people of all types, but one is most amusing.
The "No Peer" folks who strut and preen while utterly confusing
their own inflated mind's-eye view of how much they're appealing
to every single passerby—in all aspects revealing
their wholly baseless confidence that their looks radiating
mean with them everyone they meet is desirous of mating.

Those certain they are dazzling, the ones scoring near ten,
we all do run across them. It's so comical when
a rampant narcissism is on open display.
You have to laugh. Just go ahead. There is no other way.
Surely, degrees of confidence outdo feeling dejected.
But character, not arrogance, is what need be respected.

So calculate your number. I hope you score near zero.
It means you're sensible, at peace, and you would be my hero.

A Tribute to Craig

While you are a coworker difficult to tolerate,
whose conduct toward some colleagues borders on the reprobate,

another is worthy of praise. Whom do I select?
A gentle and effective soul afforded no respect.

If one person in our office has a value most profuse,
it is he with magic fingers who is paid to reproduce.

You may think his task a pure joy and covet his assignment,
for replicate he does all day with boldness and refinement.

But he is not a scoundrel, a prize stallion, or a rabbit.
He is Craig, the copy guy, with a prolific habit.

He stands before the whirring frame and issues his commands.
Unrivaled synchronicity is all that he demands.

He piles more paper in the tray and raises his skilled hand,
adjusting fearsome buttons only they two understand.

He lowers that most potent arm, presses the lever firm,
and when he lifts his arm again, the task has come to term.

He may not always get it right. He may screw up sometime.
But he remains unflappable. Device and he in rhyme.

No deadline a challenge too great. No pressure too much work.
He knows how to remain pure calm and let you go berserk.

But when the job is proper, he's a master of his fate.
Perfect stapled packets will he mystically create.

Each time Craig, the true maestro, assumes his rightful place,
the symphony begins anew, in two-sided boldface.

He makes far less money than you, lacks prospects for promotion.
But of a lesser value? Be disabused of that notion!

You're not more key than anyone, regardless of their task,
so have esteem for everyone. It's not too much to ask.

Show real appreciation for folks at every rank.
The measure of your merit is whom you take time to thank.

As you adroitly "manage up," with a deference renowned,
stop acting so superior and "manage all around."

It angers me to see disdain for Craig and his gestations.
But for him, you'd have no vapid, precious presentations.

My Turn

It must be very difficult to be so insecure,
inventing competitions simply to ensure
you've something to feel good about, some ground for a false pride,
pretending to excel just so you can others deride.

The competition you invent: who is the better human?
Declaring yourself winner, despite absent acumen.
Telling us relentlessly about each selfless deed.
A great humanitarian, a standout of our breed.

You are far more adherent in your ritual observance.
You love your children more than I or any other parents.
Your altruism's boundless. You're there for all who ask.
Endless is the gratitude in which you toil and bask.

You simply are better than me, the evidence replete.
It must be true. Why else would you unceasingly repeat
how I pale by comparison to you, ultimate giver,
with all the good and comfort you unceasingly deliver?

But if I may, oh sainted one, allow me some retort,
and be assured I say this now only as last resort.
With years of tolerating all your boasting of your glory,
permit me, for a moment, to tell you a different story.

How dare you suggest you are more honorable than I!
How dare hold your behavior somehow raises you on high!
How dare claim false comparisons to set yourself apart!
How dare feign grand morality and a more caring heart!

You know nothing about me, but you're easy to know.
Your self-image is nourished by hearing yourself crow.
You have zero accomplishments by which you've made a mark.
You act for others only for the praise the acts may spark.

"My son will be a doctor," you've told me you believe,
as if that's something *you'd* deserve the credit to achieve.
I do not think that likely. I have met your boy.
There is no profession on earth that he would less enjoy.

But if, by some turn of events, he becomes a physician,
despite glaring ineptitude for any such position,
I suggest orthopedics, so treatment you won't lack
when you dislocate your elbows patting yourself on the back.

Haywired

A work ethic is baked down deep inside our DNA,
telling us big titles come with big, rewarding pay.
We dedicate ourselves, with such unfettered attention,
to employers who seem to want our decades-long retention.

Days and nights and weekends, they warrant our devotion,
our energy, our intellect, exhaustion, every notion.
Their priorities are sacrosanct, our real lives relegated
to dwell only in margins not for business designated.

But there is always one person with an approach aberrant,
for whom such a commitment simply is not so inherent.
Someone who selects actions using wholly unique math,
deploying what's called "mindfulness" to charter their own path.

Sure, he or she may become stuck in place or even fired.
Sure, others will mock savagely one so differently wired.
But which of us is sensible and which badly misguided?
Am I both a tool and a fool? Oh damn. I've just decided.

Success in the Alternate Universe

Surmounting Aggravation More Often Than Never

Fill 'Er Up

You've now pushed enough paper
to fill a huge skyscraper.
How thoughtful of you to support
your local lumberjack.

The trees can be reseeded
but not the years you've ceded.
Wish as you may, there is no way
to get so much time back.

Before you fill a casket,
fill up a large wastebasket.
Mind-numbing rote is not the aim
of our genetic code.

Shun the date stamps and time clocks.
Toss both your in- *and* out-box.
Make paper sails, not paper trails,
to unburden the load.

I think the world would function,
even without compunction,
to fill our days with files and forms
and printouts by the ream.

Imagine creative forces,
let loose like untamed horses,
to invent and write, sculpt and debate—
perhaps fulfill a dream.

Magic Time

The magic time approaches. Reverence fills the air.
New hope springs eternal, forgotten all despair.
Thoughts turn free and happy, troubles far behind.
At once, as if divinely wrought, all is good and kind.

The magic time approaches. We'll soon alight the street
to search about the local shops to find what we might eat.
Friendships again are renewed. Companionship is found.
The power of the magic time never fails to astound.

But what is it about this time that makes our pulses thunder?
What is the source of such delight and boundless joy and wonder?
Perhaps it's the camaraderie that makes our hearts beat fast.
Perhaps it's sharing a small laugh or bits of fine repast.

But these are overshadowed by the fundamental cause
of the mystical grandeur in this universal pause.
For the fact that more than any renders magic time so dear,
is knowing for one hour we'll get the hell out of here.

Game Theory

To play the game and gain some fame, so the theory goes,
choose to use and then abuse, to score a lethal blow.

They tell me I must wheel and deal if I'm to win this race.
My only drive must be *survive*, to reach meaningful place.

I'm told, "don't feel," "abide appeal," to grab substantial power.
I need to pounce on every ounce of weakness every hour.

That is, they say, the only way, to climb the corporate ladder.
For real import I must resort to *crush, assault, and batter*.

But they don't tout the other route to feed my grand ambition.
How to surpass, though not an ass, and act without sedition.

Examples here are plain. If I am quiet, but insane,
I'll hit my stride, upward glide, and ride that gravy train.

Don't Ask Me. I Just Work Here.

We're middle-grade employees.
You think we're here to aid?
And answer all your questions?
You think *that's* why we're paid?

Need some simple info?
Think we're here to help?
Think again. No answers here,
only verbal kelp.

We'll tangle up the simplest phrase,
evade your issue quick.
We'll wrap nonsense around your ears—
pretty nifty trick.

This is, of course, what we will do
if in a giving mood.
If not, we'll send you somewhere else
to others just as rude.

You will come to know outrage.
You'll hate as ne'er before.
You'll spend time to gain nothing
but the chance to spend some more.

Methinks you just expect too much
of us here in this place.
Did you think we would answer you,
and do it face-to-face?

You should have known our honor code:
Knowledge never flaunt!
For like an ancient deadly curse,
an answer lives to haunt.

Let's Get Deep

You do one thing only and do it well.
That's how this company works.
It may be oppressive and boring as hell,
if imagination is one of your quirks.

Again and again you do one little task,
like no one else in the world could.
You may even be happy, if that's all you ask,
like a doughnut, a brick, or some wood.

You might get great at your one little job,
expert, but your vibrancy tainted.
You could be the best, stand out from the mob,
and with all else be unacquainted.

There isn't much else to say about this,
but consistent with the subject matter,
I will not move on, for then I would miss
the chance to repeat the same chatter.

No! Wait! I am not locked into this spot.
Perhaps I'll explore something new.
My mind, it need not only reprise and clot.
I'll discourse with the bold and the few.

So let us talk science and fashion that's chic,
psychology, religion, and trends.
But not all at once. I escaped just last week
and too much will give me the bends.

Daylight

It's dark when I go to work.
It's dark when I go home.
I'm told there's daylight in between.
It's like I live in Nome.

I'm told that when the daylight shines
people go outdoors.
That sometimes the air has a warmth,
even floral allures.

They say the sun when shining
reveals highlights in one's hair,
and something called "sunglasses"
may be worn to block the glare.

I'm told some backyards come alive
with children playing games
and tossing balls, playing tag,
calling others mean names.

They even say that on a beach
in sunshine you see sand,
and a horizon is revealed
wherever you may stand.

They say there are no stars out then,
but birds are seen in flight,
and all manner of colors burst
that can't be seen at night.

No, those who claim these things are wrong.
They must be out of touch.
For if there's any truth to it,
I've sacrificed too much.

I think I'll take tomorrow off,
so I can go outside
and then resume my work schedule,
assured that they have lied.

Perspective

Am I really feeling calmer or is this still hyperstress?
Is television better or am I settling for less?
Is this a decent haircut or just a controlled mess?
My relative perspective's gone. It's true, I must confess.

Is two hours a good commute because it isn't three?
Are sample products only good because they are for free?
Do I just like some kinds of cheese because they aren't brie?
My relative perspective's gone, as you plainly can see.

Do summer months seem such a treat because it isn't snowing?
Is there a logic to the phrase "Hello, I must be going"?
Have mindless years at this job made me question what I'm knowing?
My relative perspective's gone. Consequences are showing.

```
Worth a Try
```

So next time your email at work
says you are disconnected,
do not reach out to I.T.
and stare at "Password Rejected."
Get mad, fight back, defend,
revive the glory of our kind.
Rebel against our rulers.
Hit the cosmic rewind.

If you have a message
for a neighboring coworker,
don't await restoration
and sit still and go berserker.
Recall there is alternative
to electronic "send."
Challenge the current ethic—
to your will it may bend.

Move your resting buttocks
from their all-too-comfy seat
and walk to the adjoining cube,
although it's four whole feet.

Interrupt your colleague
from his game of Angry Birds,
and do what we make toddlers do:
"Try to use your words."

You'll be met with a vacant stare,
born of both fear and shock,
like the first caveman witnessing
his aunt draw with a rock.

Persist. Be brave.
He may respond
if you just hold your ground.
And that response
may take the form
of utterance of sound.

But his instinct and breeding
will prove too hard to suppress.
He may speak words in the reply
and you thusly address:

"Who are you?
Email me your name
and email what you've said."
And you'll slink back to your own cube,
your revolution dead.

There you'll await the tech folks,
perhaps a little teary,
fully grasping the sad import
of Mr. Darwin's theory.

What Do You Mean I Can't Pay with This?

I made a vault deposit
of things too long in my closet.
I'd kept them in a mason jar that only I could see.

The jar was overflowing
with treasure ever growing.
I was thrilled to secure it for the bank's nominal fee.

So my savings I tendered.
With pleasure I surrendered
my vast accumulation to enable and support

adventures up ahead in life,
great things for my children and wife,
and oh so many fine pursuits of all manner and sort.

For decades I'd practiced law
so one day I could withdraw
my sustenance for years to come, for everything we'd dreamed.

I thought I'd not get so far,
way back when I passed the bar.
Financial security truly was all it seemed.

It was worth the hours so long,
the arguing right and wrong,
worth all of the exhaustion, all the stress, struggles and doubt.

It was worth the weekends and nights,
the fierce just and unjust fights.
It was worth the all we gave it. It's what hard work was about.

Executives of each stripe,
and I say this without hype,
had told me how my diligence had turned profit from loss.

Their praise had been unanimous,
the words used so magnanimous,
heaped on me my whole career by each client and boss.

They said I deftly grew wealth,
assured their bottom-line health,
and did it all through brilliant work, consummate legal skill.

My recompense had been praise
in lieu of meaningful raise,
but that's okay, for there I sat on reserves of goodwill.

Reserves so vast, so swollen,
I'd no longer risk them stolen,
and so I put them in a vault where they'd await my spending.

Such riches at beck and call,
with pride I had earned them all,
so I could reap my due reward once an expense was pending.

My daughter, whom I adore,
so gifted, caring, much more,
soon gained admission to a fine, renowned, prestigious college.

And so the day had arrived,
the boundless joy I derived,
knowing I could afford to pay for her pursuit of knowledge.

That day's why I'd been working.
Erasing fears long lurking,
I would fulfill my goal, my most enduring life ambition.

Exhausting a large percent
of our cash, money so well spent,
I paid a fraction of the bill for the absurd tuition.

And in the mail promptly tossed
a check for one-third the cost,
with a note to the bursar most politely explaining

that the remaining two-thirds
would be paid with the grateful words
that I'd saved in my goodwill bank, the wealth I'd been retaining.

In reply to my letter,
the bursar said I'd better
remit at once the balance due in form of check or cash.

The school shocked me conveying,
that message devastating,
that it found wholly worthless my entire goodwill stash.

I'd met each job objective.
While it may be subjective,
I'd been lauded my whole career for targets I'd exceeded.

But still I couldn't afford
their school, despite my reward?
Despite the praise so unrestrained, so lofty, so repeated?

I called and spoke with the dean.
I said "What is it you mean?
Are you saying my whole life's work has been a toil for naught?"

He said, "Dear sir, I tell you,
what we need is real value.
Without money, your daughter, though deserving, won't be taught."

So all those corporate shakers
were all well-rehearsed fakers
who, at no cost to them, liberally doled out gratitude.

While I felt satisfaction
for each outcome and transaction,
thinking success, in fairness, must result from platitude.

So here I sit at square one.
What I've worked for is not won,
cash and not impressions now my only driving force.

It's good to be respected,
but don't be misdirected.
A mountain of "well-dones" supplies no meaningful recourse.

Goodwill's merit is passing,
like a tooth-pulling gassing,
meant to distract achievers while others grab the ring.

Demand cash compensation
for effort and dedication.
Praise has its place, but in the end, it won't buy a damned thing!

So I say in conclusion,
to combat your own illusion,
I hope you heed my warning and you think this poem is great.

But don't voice adoration,
that engenders aggravation.
Just send your AMEX number and the expiration date.

What Happened?

It's said to be effective you must act with even keel,
exhibiting demeanor far serener than you feel.
That calm and tempered judgment is ideal, but far too rare,
for humans daily tested being driven to despair.

Composure makes you cherished and sets you on a course
to being valued at your work, for being a great source
of logic, rationality, when all is in upheaval—
until authentic you is lost without hope of retrieval.

Money Matters

Corporate securities are riddled with impurities.
Many accounting practices are wrong, or worse, corrupt.

And bond returns grow slowly. Although some find them holy,
be they public or private, the gains are not abrupt.

Certificates of deposit beat shoe boxes in your closet,
but why tie up your funds when needs defy anticipation?

Secure yourself in real estate, as long as you don't start too late.
Sorry, but you've missed a century's appreciation.

Your savings institution claims to bring wealth to fruition,
but they'll pay you a fraction of their earnings overnight.

Or you can stuff a mattress at your value-losing address.
You'll get accumulation, if only piles of dust mites.

You could start a new venture and issue a new debenture,
but you're too good a person for the requisite behavior.

In sum, handling your assets is a task with many facets.
Despite their hype, no one's your friend or your financial savior.

There is but one solution for your fiscal stress, confusion.
Renown for smart investing will ensure you Wall Street cred.

Fold all your paper money into hats jaunty and funny.
Your epitaph will boast "At least with cash, he used his head."

Yup, I Did That!

To gossip is a sin,
per rabbinical retort.
Nowhere more than in the office,
where it's an Olympic sport.

Your colleagues are like family
and should be so regarded—
true, if all your relatives
are scheming and hard-hearted.

This group selects its weaponry
unrestrained by civil code,
taking constant, careful aim,
while acting in stealth mode.

Beware of this, your family,
whose tongues will not be still,
who slander, rumor, invent tales
to stoke their gossip mill.

They'll laugh about your competence,
impugn your moral thread.
They'll craft the most malicious lies,
so others are misled.

They'll denigrate your fashion choice,
the way you comb your hair,
the friends you see outside of work,
from angles most unfair.

They'll say your ethics are a joke.
Your nature they'll debase,
and do so where you can't defend,
and never face-to-face.

They'll keep up the pounding drumbeat,
of things wild and untrue,
until claiming a victory
when they have ruined you.

And you'll not know about it,
till snippets reach your ears,
and all that you have worked to build
is laid low by their smears.

But I've a way to fight them.
It's foolproof, I must say.
Resist the great temptation.
Remain above the fray.

Approach the watercooler,
but only for a drink.
Do not talk about others.
Don't whisper with a wink.

And when you hear the gossip,
their slanderous refrain,
the things they say about you,
steadfast you must remain.

Admit to everything they say.
Proudly claim they're real,
and they'll move on to someone else,
as truth has no appeal.

Tell them the heinous things they claim
are things that you have done.
Turn all their lies into the truth,
and you'll undo their fun.

And as an added bonus,
they'll think you're weird as hell
and be afraid to speak your name,
as in you demons dwell.

Such gossipers are offspring
of those fathers and mothers
who are not like the rest of us.
In fact, they're like few others.

It's an unholy union
most people would eschew,
for it produces people
with tragically low IQ.

When humans mate with doorknobs,
their children do not know
right from wrong or truth from lies
or even friend from foe.

But there rests our assurance
we'll defeat gossip and scandal.
For doorknobs' children, luckily,
all are easy to handle.

Yeah, Let's Go with That

Since childhood I have dreamed
of doing what, it seemed,
would help all of humankind reach new heights.

I studied and I tested,
and every peer I bested,
advancing, learning, gaining new insights.

Each bad or worse employment,
mere strategic deployment,
as I drew ever nearer to my goal.

And with fifty rotations
around Sol, great jubilations!
I have attained contentment in my soul.

What is it I have worked toward?
What now has brought this reward
of knowing how unselfishly I've served?

It has been doing my best
at my wealthy clients' behest
to ensure they keep riches they don't deserve.

As counsel to corporations,
I devote my inspirations
to those who are amassing vast estates.

I endure imbroglios
to ensure their portfolios
grow and diversify at rousing rates.

These cherished one-percenters
needing jobs? Becoming renters?
I'll let no such injustices hold sway.

So please share with me my pride,
along my daily train ride,
as I think of all the good I've done that day.

And now you know my story,
a career steeped in glory.
Society, you're welcome, from my heart.

So it should be no mystery
that revisionist history
is yet one more skill I've honed to fine art.

One Approach

Never make a decision.
It would only imperil your fate.
You'd be the subject of derision.
Your prospects will lie in state.

Never display insight.
It would only unnerve your boss,
who himself radiates dim light,
and advanced on mental moss.

Never be assertive.
It would only bring you down.
Most will think you're furtive,
others that you're a clown.

Never seek achievement.
There the greatest dangers rest.
It would only bring bereavement.
Learn mediocrity is best.

Don't strive to be a hero,
and you'll doubtless survive.
You may be a pointless zero,
but your career may be alive.

Office-Adjacent and Nonadjacent

Other Things That Need to be Said

A Good Day!

Uncork the champagne! Sweet victory is yours!
Revel in the acclaim, as the finest bubbly pours.
Months of trial are over. The hours were so long.
Glory in the moment, and sing out the victor's song:

Everybody!
                        "We crushed opposing counsel.
                        We once thought him our peer.
                        We made him look so foolish.
                        We ended his career.

                        Our client now is happy.
                        We've garnered our full pay.
                        The jury pursued justice,
                        but we won anyway!"

Battleground

Uneasy suspicion stifles the air.
Foreboding glances dart.
Fear and aggression play grim and bare.
It's the deli counter at the mart.

Clawing and shoving—New York rules of thumb.
Abuse one another at will.
Throw someone down like an aging breadcrumb.
Never, but never, stand still.

Animals, fish, sometimes only a head,
lie motionless, some without bones.
Animals, human, civility shed,
more violent than some Game of Thrones.

Folks move through the crowd right to the first,
like scalpels held by a great surgeon.
But ligaments torn? Unrivaled bloodthirst?
All for a half pound of sturgeon?

The "next number" dispenser might help, you may say,
while orderly waiting your turn.
Wrong! The most skillful will still cause a fray,
in ways the naïve can't discern.

They pick up used numbers they find on the floor,
asserting that now it's their time.
The numbers are doubtless from rounds gone before,
for many, the real gateway crime.

I'd rather eat noodles, detergent, or eggs,
less sought after things in a box.
It's better than suffering two broken legs
for the glory of eating some lox.

Manifesto

To egress from Boston's Back Bay Station,
for thousands commuting by rail transportation,
there is a wide staircase fitting two abreast
and attached escalator for those needing rest.

Displayed is behavior both odd and disturbing,
a daily ritual amusing, unnerving,
actions revealing distorted perspectives
on how to prioritize one's life objectives.

Escalating, it seems, has inviolable code
for how to pass others also on that road,
an ethic revered by all humans who travel,
thread of social fabric no one dare unravel.

If you want to just stand, advanced by machine,
the right side's the side for being serene.
The left's an express lane if keen on improving
commute time. Walk up? *The thing's already moving!*

Woe unto you if by bad luck or fate,
press of crowd, ignorance, sedition innate,
you find yourself left side, but still and contented,
tasking the device for which it was invented.

You'll be an object of outrage from behind,
assumed asinine, or more, displaced of mind.
You'll hear "Move aside!" and "Get out of my way!"
from those whose import compels they rush the day.

But what's so precious to those pressing ahead,
to add their momentum to that of the tread?
How vital, really, are the seconds they gain?
Does thinking them crucial prove they are insane?

Enough! I say. My rights will now be asserted,
and you left-lane pushers be hereby alerted.
No more those who escalate as God intended
will sheepishly squeeze right for fear you're offended.

We'll stand right, center, left—where'er we damn please!
Enjoy the sights, ride, and get on/off with ease.
Impeding your progress? We'll do so with pride.
We'll not suffer arrogance. We *won't* step aside.

You think the world enriched by the seconds you gain.
Your need to pass me makes that ever so plain.
So I say, with respect, as I also pay fares,
I am not impressed. Take the freakin' stairs!

Love Thyself

Thirty-seven people vie for one Assembly seat.
All, certain that they will prevail, with confidence compete.

Some think they're the smartest. Intellect will out.
Some think contacts are the key. They rely on clout.
Some think they're best looking. Electorates vote looks.
Some think they're the wealthiest. First place for balanced books.
Some think they're most eloquent. Turned phrases rule the day.
Some think they're most decent. Good nature carries sway?
Some think they're a privileged lot, born to sure success.
Others, acting "colorfully," use gimmicks, they'll confess.
First-timers push their greenness. People like what's new.
Old-timers stress experience. They're like a worn-in shoe.
Some aggressive candidates insult, bully the field.
And some know, if they are to win, it's compromise and yield.

Just one will reach the pinnacle and revel in first place.
The question is how to predict which one will win the race.

The formula is simple, reliable, and trite
to forecast who will not be conceding election night.
The most successful person can look in mirrored glass
and see each trait cited above, while you just see an ass.

The Office Softball Dynasty

Another summer closes, yet fall cannot displace
the still fantastic visions of athleticism, grace
indelibly imprinted on the very privileged few
lucky to have witnessed the exploits of Team 2.

Sure, our skills all have regressed from when we were just lads.
Sure, we wrench and pull muscles we never knew we had.
Sure, we fracture body parts and tear what cannot break.
Sure, we must remove our socks to count errors we make.

But we are first in spirit! That is at our core.
Would we have more fun if we could win a little more?
Perhaps. But we'll let others revel in their softball skills
and be content at game time to have executed wills.

Recall 2007, when a great Patriots team
was on the cusp of fulfilling their loyal fans' great dream,
by dispatching, convincingly, each and every foe
and capturing an unblemished nineteen wins in a row.

Just before the Super Bowl, attorneys for Bob Kraft
were given a retainer to a short petition draft,
to trademark a signature phrase. They understood the reason
for wanting to protect "19 and 0, The Perfect Season."

I suggest we get a copy of those papers filed,
so we can monetize the awesome record *we've* compiled.
For we've achieved ineptness with historical perfection,
finishing 19 and 0, but not in that direction.

So here's to you, my teammates, intrepid, proud, and game.
We share a rare, transcendent bond that others cannot claim.
We, as a team, truly believe that having fun is winning,
and we hold fast to that as we endure each twelve-run inning.

Metal Box

A metal box, recessed light,
oblivious to day or night,
soars above the open pit.
To faith in physics I submit
and enter the carpeted floor,
endure the clash of steely door.
Gravity arouses fear,
with motion born of grinding gear.
Numbers flash, a scraping heard.
I face the front without a word.
Hours seem but seconds true.
Pulse pounding, I await my cue.
And then, despite the stories high,
I get a sense I may not die.
Suddenly more steely doors.
They break apart and light assures
I won't need a defibrillator.
Man, I hate this elevator!

Let's Tie One On

Who was the ass who invented men's ties?
And who the moron who epiphanied, "My,
wouldn't it be just fashion at its height,
if all men in offices wore lassos pulled tight
with knots to ensure extreme oxygen loss,
smashing Adam's apples into applesauce?"

But I wonder who is the much bigger jerk,
the inventor or each sheep who wears them to work?
I think that my mirror shows me the real dope
who every day matches his suit to his rope.

One day as my leash bore deep into my neck,
to blot out the pain, I took time to reflect
on some use for which the tie may have been born,
since it's idiotic if meant to adorn.

I traveled, I researched, I pored over books.
Without food, I camped out in library nooks.
Ten years I devoted my all to the quest,
how choking and sweating mark me as well dressed.

And then to profound satisfaction and awe,
I came on the answer I so long searched for.
From a most obscure text, in Italian dialect,
I learned that a man's tie was meant to protect.

It's really an elegant safety device
to prevent a real harm and preserve human life.

Imperial Rome was inventive at heart,
with aqueducts, archways, and towering art—
structures so complex it is hard to believe
the heights ancient thinkers and craftsmen achieved.

If you overlook the mad emperor-kings,
plundering, blood sport, a few other things,
you may regard Rome as a source of some good.
In fact, my new findings reveal that you should.

For Romans invented the indoor commode,
an oval device in each wealthy abode,
a water exchanger to eliminate mess,
a great new advance for those flushed with success.

But toilets of Rome were a double-edged sword.
Handy, but like rivers far too deep to ford,
many of the empire's young men of renown
routinely fell in and were tragically drowned.

So orders went forth to the greatest of minds,
a handsome reward set for one who could find
a way to avert such unseemly demise,
a way to warn men of unsafe water rise.

A genius, now unknown, brought his idea forth:
a long, narrow, tapering piece of bright cloth
that you would wrap tightly around your own throat,
on one end a small stone unable to float.

And then, before using your new mechanism,
you'd dip it to see if the water had risen.

If the cloth came out merely wet at the tip,
"Proceed with your task, but please try not to slip."
If the cloth came out wet halfway up to its height,
"Proceed, but use caution. You'd better sit tight!"
If the cloth came out wet up to where it was tied,
"Danger! Beware! Take your business outside!"

In this way, the tie, a design so sublime,
its brilliance and purpose once lost for all time,
like fire, the wheel, the men's tie by its birth
sustained humankind as a species on Earth.

And though women then were thought less smart and brave,
Rome also deemed them somewhat worthy to save.
A great new contraption was a megahit
that let women also find out when to sit.

A concept employed by women 'round the globe,
twisty bits of metal that hung from earlobes.
It's why even to this day our wives and our daughters
affix dangling earrings and dab "toilet waters."

So let us rethink just how foolish the tie.
It kept our whole species regular and dry.
The next time you lean in a bathroom too dim,
and your tie or your earring goes in for a swim,
be grateful to Romans between mumbled curse,
for drowning in toilets was probably worse.

Introduction to "The Motor Pool"

For the uninitiated, a "motor pool" is a collection of cars maintained by a company or government agency for use by employees for local business travel. Most people, however, do not know the term derives from famed "camel pools" of ancient Egypt.

The earliest mention of a camel pool appears in a hieroglyph dated to 1141 BCE. It was created to log the work of the Egyptian Bureau of Mirage Management. In addition to mentioning the pool, the tablet records the not-at-all surprising frustration of bureau employees attempting site visits.

One renowned modern thinker—okay, yours truly—posits that automobiles traversed ancient Egypt. Evidence is irrefutable. For example, we now know the word "caravan" appearing throughout the Bible has been misinterpreted for millennia. In ancient Hebrew, the letter "a" or "aleph" appearing at the mathematical center of a word should be read as the conjunction "or." Finally, we understand what Joseph was asking when he inquired, "Is that a car-avan I see approaching from Midian?" You would think that during two thousand years of biblical scholarship, someone before me might have spotted that.

Another modern intellectual—okay, me again—theorizes that automobiles of ancient Egypt were nothing like today's vehicles. They, in fact, were motorized camels known throughout the ancient world as "dune buggies." For proof, we need look no further than a recently discovered pharaonic obelisk bearing an inscription loosely translated as:

Expect delays 5 a.m. to 8 a.m. at watering holes. During plod hours, one-humpers prohibited from express lanes. Hands-free devices only. Pharoah wishes you a pleasant flood season.

But I digress. Back to modern times. I never will forget the inspiring motto stenciled on the wall of my company's motor pool: *Safety First—Counting Backwards.*

The Motor Pool

Only official business can justify a car
and *only if V.P.s sign off*. It is kind of bizarre.
Calling these junkpiles "cars" is a charitable refrain,
as typically they will not move beyond their own oil stain.

At least they could be courteous, giving you these fakes
that play at being vehicles but have no lights or brakes.
But no, they are the rudest lot as they roll out your prize,
assuring you of safety, expediting your demise.

They are supposed to fill the tank before you can pull out,
but these guys only fill 'em up for people with real clout.
The rest of us have to contend with needles below red
and fear the smell is from a year-old lunch or something dead.

Consider yourself wholly blessed if the radio works,
and think of rearview mirrors as more unexpected perks.
If there's a windshield wiper and the switch works on the dash,
lucky you, at least you'll see the bus before you crash.

No wonder that a motor pool is where all this is run.
These cars and pools often have both been used for "number one."
Or maybe the name's telling you it isn't yet too late.
Pool your funds. Buy a car. You're only tempting fate.

Most likely the term "motor pool" reflects the troubling feeling
that your garage encounter is reliably revealing.
For when beneath the motor you observe a "pool" of glop,
you'll know that when you hit the brake, only your heart will stop.

Lunchroom

A soda machine and one with canned juice.
That's all it has—no food. What's the use
of a lunchroom that has no food to sell
but still somehow offers that old lunchroom smell?
A room with some chairs and a table or two.
A place to have people drop things on your shoe.
A place to see people unpack those brown bags
and discover what lurks in aluminum rags.
A place to meet folks you did not want to see,
where talk may be cheap, but the nausea is free.
The lunchroom, a pointless misuse of good space,
where you play "Let's identify food on his face."
A room where it's tough to be always polite,
while insides are searching for lost appetite.
I've no doubt that even were it all blown up,
the scent would linger of stale Sprite in a cup.

Introduction to
"The Company Medical Office"

The overwhelming majority of medical doctors are intelligent and caring, dedicated to the well-being of all. They are disciples of Hippocrates, people to whom the oath they pronounced upon graduation has enduring significance. A few, however, disdain the teachings of Hippocrates and adhere, instead, to those of Hippocrates's lesser-known cousin, Hypocrisies. To these so-called "Hypocrites," a "living" is something they fraudulently earn, although *living* is not what they help you do. I encountered these doctors in a company medical office.

On taking my first job with a big enterprise, I was assured the tale I tell in "The Company Medical Office" had taken place. Nothing in my experience there persuaded me otherwise.

The Company Medical Office

For our medical group, let's have cheers—
for doctors without active careers,
who work for this place
to avoid the disgrace
of no income, no talent, no peers.

Legend of the group lives today,
which is more than their patients can say.
They're a last resort.
The coroner's report
will follow as night follows day.

It never will cease to astound,
how each diagnosis is found.
Complain of a cough?
They'll lance a wart off,
and soon you're ensconced underground.

Come in complaining of ache?
They'll assume you are a fake.
You say it's your toes.
They'll say it's your nose.
You won't smell a thing at your wake.

The story is told of a Chet,
who of much leg discomfort did fret.
He told of his pain.
They X-rayed his brain,
as part of their usual set.

The brain X-ray showed something dread,
a large tumor grown in his head.
They said his demise
should be no surprise.
In three months he'd surely be dead.

So Chet went and told his dear wife
of his soon-to-be too-shortened life.
He put money aside
for the kids when he died
and coped with unrelenting strife.

Three months passed, but poor Chet did not.
Then four months, and then quite a lot.
Emotionally wrought,
he reasonably sought
new doctors to see what was what.

The new doctors said Chet was great.
No longer for death should he wait.
They suggested one thing:
"Give those doctors a ring
and inquire why they sealed your fate."

So Chet phoned the medical pack
and told them disease he did lack.
Saying, "I am alive.
Your diagnosis was jive.
How was it you got so off track?"

The doctors then looked into that
and found when for X-rays Chet sat,
they'd failed to discover
his religious headcover
and diagnosed "terminal hat."

Even if ill in the extreme,
don't go to that medical team!
Rush to the front door.
Don't suffer still more.
Find doctors with some self-esteem.

Payback

Advanced degrees allow you to make lifetime contributions.
Regrettably, they're made to debt-servicing institutions.

They say, "Now there's a student whose commitment will not fade,
as evidenced by study through the twenty-seventh grade."

And armed with your degrees, you'll research, teach, and enhance knowledge,
far better than those ne'er-do-wells who only went to college.

I don't knock education. It drives civilization.
But loan repayment currency should be great inspiration.

Keep It to Yourself, Will Ya?

I remember not so long ago
that passwords were for spies,
and pins were used to hold my dress shirts
firmly to my ties.
Now I'm known by secret IDs.
It just does not make sense.
To L.L. Bean, I'm "Donut,"
to Amazon, "Dog Fence."
And as for my PIN structures,
the limits reach the sky.
Some are just fifteen digits,
but others rival pi.

Where did it all go crazy
with the numbers and the words,
alphanumeric jumbles
so identities are blurred?
Don't use a common name or date, especially your birth,
for surely then the cyber creeps
take you for all you're worth.

Passwords must be sequences
no one could ever guess.
The best are those that come across
as random, meaningless.
Even though you must employ
a long, senseless array,
make sure you still recall it
at least ten times every day.

And though you must remember it,
writing it brings a curse.
You'll risk your deepest secrets
flashing 'round the universe.

I can't do much about this.
It's far bigger than me,
for I'm reduced to numbers
and bizarre words on some keys.
But it's okay. I get along.
It's a great modern day.
I'll gain access with "$umpPump,"
and next month, "Che3seOl@y."

Who Cares?

I'm waiting for the train.
Of course, it's not on time.
That gives me all the time I need
to ponder station grime.

People all around me
are whipping out cell phones,
a symphony of buttons pushed,
soothing harmonic tones.

Talk jumbles as they inform
that they'll arrive too late
for their vital appointments.
The meetings have to wait.

I am not that important.
I need not make a call.
If I am a few minutes late,
nobody cares at all.

My minutes are not crucial.
I'll not each second seethe.
I can afford simply to sit
and read and think and breathe.

I'm waiting for the train.
Of course, it's not on time.
I'm a total non-player.
Isn't life sublime?

You Want Jam on That?

Each day the sun rises anew,
and we may not be here, it's true.
Big picture stuff can't be foreseen,
so on mundane matters we lean,
to give false sense of mastery
and quell fears of disastery.

So we must make small acts routine,
for from them some control we glean.
Finding comfort, we take no chance.
We brush our teeth, put on our pants.
We grab the train, endure delays,
and we curse our smartphone displays.
We switch on lights, the CPU,
and read the spam that still got through.
We eat some lunch. We give advice.
We find it hard to be so nice.
We shut the door, rehop the train,
endure delays, shut off our brain,
have dinner, chat, half-eye the news,
and feel that day we've paid our dues.
Brush teeth. Oh look, it's half past ten!
Tomorrow? Let's do this again!

We can't predict the speeding bus,
the dread disease, the feud and fuss.
We can't foresee a street attack,
a sudden storm, getting the sack.
We can't know when love will be spent,

a trust betrayed, injustice meant.
We can't predict things of import.
Oh well. *So what!* That's my retort.

We rule the things that we do next,
like do I stop or write more text?
Like do I turn to left or right?
Like do I paint this wall off-white?

These are the things we *can* decide,
like do I want that baked or fried?
Or for which sports team should I root?
Or does this hat make me look cute?
As long as we can choose our pie,
who needs a say in when we die?

All that we do matters. Why else are we here?
Don't fret that you're not in control. Relax and be of cheer.
Be glad that we are masters of the things that matter most.
Wouldn't you rather choose to *eat*, and not when you'll *be*, toast?

Acknowledgments

Thank you to Paula for allowing me to vent to you via these poems as I have written them throughout my career. Thank you also for laughing at parts I intended to be funny, and sagely advising and supporting me as we navigated the frustrations catalogued in this collection.

Thank you to our highly accomplished children Sarah and Josh for your valuable feedback and suggestions.

Thank you also to the very few friends with whom I shared parts of this volume as it neared completion. Your enjoyment of them and their relatability to your own experiences, as well as your comments and criticisms, were key in helping get across the finish line.

Thank you to the handful of work colleagues with whom I shared selections in recent years. As we endured certain aggravations together, I thought you also might be comforted by my mocking them. I am gratified you were.

Thank you to Dara Syrkin, an invaluable copy editor. I appreciate your insight, ear, and sensibilities as you reviewed my manuscript and made suggestions to ensure readers would glean my intent on every line—and in proper cadence.

Thank you to Jess LaGreca of Mayfly for your creativity and skill in designing the look and layout of this book. Thank you also to Julie Scheife and Ryan Scheife of Mayfly for your guidance and technical assistance throughout the publication process.

Thank you to Stuart McReath for your cover illustration replicated throughout the volume. You captured my vision to a degree I had not thought possible. Your artistic talent, collaborative style and dedication to craft give my words wonderful visual dimension and I am grateful for the opportunity to have worked with you.

Thank you to Marcy and Harry, my parents, who were relentlessly devoted to ensuring my brother and I were happy, cared for, and well-educated. Uplifted by our nurturing environment, my brother and I became the first generation in our family to attend college, let alone attain professional degrees. I've wondered whether my love of words, and what can happen when you string them together, was a product of our family's lack of money. Early on, I recognized that words were available for free and, if deployed to their potential, could be a great equalizer for people not bequeathed wealth or influence.

Thank you also to my grandfather Dan for many things, but particularly for the following three lessons about respect:

1. Every person deserves a baseline amount of my respect simply for being another human.
2. People can earn greater respect from me only if they demonstrate commitment to integrity and justice. They can, and should, forfeit my respect if their actions do not evidence genuine commitment to those principles.
3. Nothing other than fidelity to those principles warrants respect above the "you're another human being" threshold—not position, title, family or educational pedigree, wealth, appearance, fame, influence—and certainly not the confidence or arrogance with which any of those "advantages" may be asserted.

Finally, I want to thank the most arrogant, obnoxious, and expensively dressed person I've ever met. A brief story.

On graduating law school, many classmates took sought-after, ridiculously high-paying jobs with fancy firms. I did not. I decided to pay back the

New York City public school system for the foundation it had provided me and took a job as litigation counsel in the office of its chancellor. My responsibilities included bringing administrative charges and then trying those cases, seeking termination of tenured employees, or lesser penalties, for all sorts of misconduct ranging from criminal behavior to excessive lateness.

Every employee I charged, but one, retained union counsel, at no cost to them, for their defense. The one who did not, a teacher I charged with inappropriate behavior with a student, hired the most experienced, high-profile, highly paid defense attorney in New York City.

One winter's day during my first year on the job, that attorney came storming into our office and up to my desk. My first thought, as I sat there in my affordably cheap polyester suit, was that his long, camel hair topcoat, with its richly colored plush velvet collar, was the best-looking piece of clothing I had ever seen. My second thought was that it likely cost more than my entire wardrobe since birth.

Then he said this:

"How dare you bring these charges against my client! They are a lie. I'll make a fool of you at trial. Who do you think you are, treating her this way? What are you—a new law school graduate? I demand you withdraw these charges immediately and apologize to her and her family. I know everyone who matters in this city—on a first-name basis. Know this for certain. If you do not withdraw these charges and apologize, I will destroy your career before it even starts." He went on like that for some minutes.

I did not interrupt. I remained expressionless throughout the tirade and thought back to what my grandfather had taught me.

When the attorney finished, his smug bearing revealed his certainty that I had been intimidated and was ready, even desperate, to voice contrition. I responded as follows:

"Thanks for coming by. It's useful that you have—and nice coat, by the way. Within a day, I will send you a copy of a piece of evidence. I guarantee that, within twenty-four hours thereafter, you will call to tell me your client is resigning. Thanks again for dropping by."

Incensed, he resumed his harangue before storming out. Later that day I sent him a copy of a note his client had given the student, unquestionably confirming the allegation. Within an hour, he called and very politely informed me his client would resign.

There, at my first law job, I learned great fun could be had by facing down arrogance and the bogus superiority on which it relies. I also learned that some people have really nice coats.

About the Author

A. Martin Block has conducted and overseen civil litigation on behalf of corporations and the government for more than forty years. He served as litigation director for the world's largest municipal agency, as a partner in a national law firm, and as chief in-house trial counsel to an international enterprise. In each role, he gained unique insights into large organizations, their management, and the people without whom neither could function. He and his wife Paula live in a Boston suburb.

www.blockpoetry.com

Photo by Allie Photo